Nakano Takeko

Women of War - Book 8
History Nerds

While every precaution has been taken in the preparation of this book, the publisher assumes no responsibility for errors or omissions, or for damages resulting from the use of the information contained herein.
Nakano Takeko
Women of War - Book 8
Copyright © 2024 History Nerds.
Written by History Nerds.

Table of Contents

Introduction

Who Was Nakano Takeko?

What motivated Nakano Takeko, a fearless female warrior, to stand strong against overwhelming odds? Her very name evokes images of courage, defiance, and an unbreakable spirit. But who was the woman behind this legend?

To understand Takeko, we must first examine the world she lived in. She was born in 1847 in Edo (modern-day Tokyo), when Japan stood on the brink of upheaval. The samurai class that had ruled for centuries faced obsolescence as Western influence grew. Meanwhile, women endured expectations to be docile, subservient, and confined to domestic roles. Takeko carved an extraordinary path in this context.

As the daughter of a high-ranking official, she gained access to education and martial arts training typically reserved for men. Takeko excelled in literary arts, military strategy, sword fighting, and archery. However, she yearned to put these skills into practice and prove a woman could be as fierce and capable as any male warrior.

The crux of Takeko's story lies in her refusal to be defined or limited by societal gender expectations. In an era when passivity and demureness were demanded of women, Takeko was bold, assertive, and unapologetically fierce. She challenged the notion that valor on the battlefield belonged solely to men.

This defiance manifested fully during the Boshin War of 1868, a civil conflict pitting the ruling shogunate against those seeking to restore the emperor's power. Loyal to the emperor, Takeko and her family fought this war. In its crucible, Takeko forged her legend.

Rather than shying away, she embraced the fight. Takeko rallied and trained a group of female warriors, an unprecedented move in Japan. Her "Women's Army" shattered misconceptions that women lacked the strength, toughness, and aggression for battle. They proved every bit as disciplined, skilled, and courageous as male troops.

Takeko inspired fierce devotion through her leadership and indomitable will. Her warriors followed her out of genuine respect and belief in her cause. She led from the front, always ready to charge into the fray alongside them.

This supreme loyalty faced its ultimate test at the Battle of Aizu, where Takeko and her outnumbered, outgunned warriors defended their homeland. Eyewitnesses describe her calmly firing arrows as bullets flew around her. Gravely wounded, Takeko knew death loomed but remained concerned for her family's honor and warriors' safety. With her last breath, she asked her sister to behead her so enemies could not claim her head as a trophy. This final, fiercely independent act captured her uncompromising spirit.

Nakano Takeko was a warrior, leader, sister, and embodiment of courage. Above all, she was a trailblazer. When society expected women to be passive homemakers, she carved her own path. Takeko proved a woman could wield a sword and lead troops into battle as skillfully as any man. She faced death unflinchingly for her beliefs.

Her legacy lives on as inspiration worldwide, reminding us greatness knows no gender and bravery has many faces. Takeko defied her time's conventions, becoming a timeless icon of female empowerment. As we explore her extraordinary life's details in the following chapters, we'll see how she defined herself on her own terms, leaving an indelible mark on history.

Samurai Spirit: Unveiling the Bushido

To truly appreciate Nakano Takeko's remarkable journey, we must first understand the guiding principles that shaped her world and actions - the Bushido code. More than just rules, Bushido embodied the very soul of the samurai warrior. It elevated duty, honor, and loyalty above all else. As we explore the intricacies of this code, we'll discover the foundation upon which Takeko built her legendary life.

Bushido, often translated as "the way of the warrior," evolved over centuries as a fluid philosophy. Its roots trace back to feudal Japan when samurai pledged allegiance to lords in exchange for land and status. Over time, these warriors developed unique values that set them apart from ordinary citizens.

At its core, Bushido emphasized unwavering loyalty to one's master - a bond transcending mere duty into the sacred realm. A samurai's word was an unbreakable bond. Breaking an oath invited dishonor and shame. This devotion often meant a willingness to sacrifice one's life for their lord, a concept known as "seppuku" or ritual suicide.

But loyalty alone did not define the samurai spirit. Bushido also prized courage, both physical and moral. Samurai faced any challenge, whether on the battlefield or in personal life, with unflinching bravery. This courage was not the absence of fear but the ability to act despite it - to do what was right even when consequences seemed dire.

Intertwined with courage was the notion of honor - a complex tapestry woven from threads of integrity, respect, and self-discipline. A samurai's honor was their most precious possession, guarded at all costs. It encompassed not only their own actions but the reputation of their family and clan. Losing honor was a fate worse than death.

Yet Bushido focused not solely on martial prowess and battlefield glory. It also emphasized cultivating the mind and pursuing knowledge. Many samurai were accomplished poets, calligraphers, and scholars, seeing no contradiction between the sword and the brush. This balance of martial and cultural arts created well-rounded warriors capable of defending their lord and contributing to society's artistic legacy.

Most fascinating is how Bushido viewed death. To the samurai, death was not to be feared but embraced as an inevitable part of life. Warriors always remained prepared to die, whether in battle or by their own hand, if it meant preserving their honor and integrity. This casual acceptance of mortality imbued samurai with fearlessness and liberation, allowing them to live each moment to the fullest.

It's crucial to understand that Bushido was not a monolithic code followed uniformly. Each clan and individual warrior interpreted and applied these principles uniquely, creating a rich tapestry of ideals that varied across time and place.

For Nakano Takeko, born into great upheaval, Bushido provided a compass for navigating her shifting world. As the daughter of a samurai family, she absorbed these values from a young age through legendary tales of warriors and the teachings of wise masters.

But Takeko did not simply accept Bushido as given; she interrogated it, molded it, and made it her own. In a society often relegating women to the sidelines, she dared ask: why should the warrior's way be limited by gender? Why couldn't a woman embody the ideals of loyalty, courage, and honor that defined the samurai?

Through her actions and leadership, Takeko challenged and expanded the notion of following the Bushido code. She proved a woman could not only uphold these values but elevate them to new heights. In rallying her Women's Army, she created a new model of the samurai embracing women's strength and potential.

Chapter 1: Aegis of Aizu

1868 was a year of great upheaval in Japan. The Emperor sought to regain power from the shogun and propel the nation into modern times. However, one domain refused to yield - the proud and defiant Aizu.

At the heart of this resistance stood the remarkable woman samurai named Nakano Takeko. Raised in a family steeped in martial traditions, Takeko mastered the warrior's ways, shattering expectations of what a woman could achieve. As war loomed, her unwavering loyalty and formidable skills faced the ultimate test.

Takeko was not alone. She found kindred spirits in other Aizu samurai women, united by fierce devotion to their domain and the Bushido code. Together, they formed the groundbreaking Jōshitai or "Women's Army" - a unit that would leave an indelible mark on history.

In autumn 1868, Imperial forces marched on Aizu. Outnumbered and outgunned, Takeko and her comrades stood as the last line of defense for their castle and way of life. Lesser warriors might have quailed, but the women of the Jōshitai met this trial with steely resolve.

Takeko's strategic acumen shone as she organized the elite Jōshitai force. Recognizing traditional tactics would fail against modern weapons, she adapted. Leveraging intimate terrain knowledge, she waged a guerrilla campaign to sap the enemy's strength and morale.

Under Takeko's leadership, the Jōshitai staged daring night raids and ambushes. They targeted supply lines, burning provisions and vanishing before the enemy could respond. Each strike bolstered their confidence while sowing fear among Imperial ranks.

But Takeko knew raids alone could not win. She aimed to win the hearts and minds of Aizu's people. The Jōshitai became symbols of hope inspiring citizens to resist by any means. Farmers, merchants, young and old - all rallied behind these extraordinary warrior women.

As the weeks dragged on, the toll grew heavy. The Imperial Army tightened its siege, determined to starve Aizu into submission. Within the castle, supplies dwindled and disease spread. Yet Takeko and the Jōshitai's resolve only hardened, embodying the unbreakable spirit of Bushido.

The pivotal moment came in October at the Battle of Aizu. With the castle's fall imminent, Takeko led a daring charge into Imperial lines. Brandishing her naginata, she fought with ferocity that struck terror into the enemy. Though beaten back wave after wave, even the mightiest samurai could not stand forever against such odds.

As the battle crested, a fatal bullet struck Takeko in the chest. Yet even in her final moments, she embodied the code that guided her life. With her last breath, she implored her sister to behead her, ensuring her body would not dishonor the enemy's hands - a final defiant act of loyalty.

Though Aizu fell, the Jōshitai's valiant stand echoed through ages. They showed the world Bushido's true meaning - that courage, honor and devotion transcend gender. Shattering the notion that a woman's place was solely in the home, they paved the way for future generations to redefine societal roles.

The Battle of Aizu stands as a testament to the power of the human spirit. Against impossible odds, Takeko and her sisters fought not just for their domain, but their very right to live by their code. They proved the warrior's way was not limited by gender, but defined by one's character and resolve.

The total number of casualties caused by the Jōshitai is not precisely recorded in historical sources, but their contribution to the battle is noted for its bravery and the symbolic importance of their resistance. The Jōshitai's efforts, though ultimately overwhelmed by the larger and better-equipped Imperial forces, are remembered for their courage and dedication.

As we reflect on this pivotal moment, we must ask: what drives us to take a stand against adversity? What principles do we hold so dear to give our full devotion? The women of Aizu offer a shining example of courage against overwhelming odds. They remind us true strength lies not in force or weapons, but in unbreakable comradeship and shared purpose.

Nakano Takeko's legacy endures as an inspiration to live with honor and purpose. Her story invites us to examine the codes guiding our lives. It challenges us to stand firm in our beliefs, even against currents of change. Most of all, it reminds us that greatness lies within each of us, if only we have the courage to seize it.

Warrior Women of the World

History's annals celebrate warriors and generals who shaped the world through their battlefield prowess. More often than not, these legends are men. However, women have also wielded the instruments of war with valor and skill that matched or surpassed their male counterparts. The brave Nakano Takeko and her fearless Jōshitai sisters charged into Imperial lines, offering just one example of remarkable female heroines. Their legacy echoes in the stories of exceptional warrior women across cultures and eras.

What unites these female fighters across time and geography? What parallels can we draw between their battles and triumphs? By examining the lives and deeds of history's most renowned women warriors, we uncover powerful themes of courage, defiance, and indomitable spirit that bind them together.

Consider Boudica, the Iceni Queen who led a massive Celtic uprising against Roman occupation in 1st Century Britain. Like Nakano Takeko, a fierce loyalty to her people and refusal to submit to unjust rule drove her. Facing a mightier, better-equipped enemy, both women adopted unconventional tactics to even the odds. Boudica's chariot charges struck terror into the disciplined Roman ranks, just as Takeko's guerrilla raids sapped Imperial morale.

Leap forward to the 15th Century and meet Joan of Arc, the peasant girl who rallied a battered French army to improbable victories against the English. Joan, like Takeko, shattered all notions of a woman's place being solely in the home. They proved greatness knows no gender in an age when female leaders were scarce. Their ability to inspire and lead men into battle stands as a testament to their fortitude and unshakeable belief.

The 19th Century Mino warriors of Benin offer perhaps the most striking parallel to Nakano's Jōshitai. This all-female military regiment guarded the Dahomey King and astounded European observers with their fearlessness and combat proficiency. Like the women of Aizu, the Mino resisted colonial incursions and fought ferociously to preserve their way of life. These warrior women became symbols of resistance and unbending resolve.

Yet each heroine arose from a unique cultural context that shaped her struggle. Boudica's uprising fueled personal loss and outrage at Roman cruelty toward her family. Joan's visions propelled her improbable victories, while Bushido's code colored Takeko's every action. The Mino drew strength from spiritual beliefs and martial traditions.

These differences underscore a truth - valor and martial skill belong to no single culture or belief system. The way of the warrior found expression in myriad forms throughout history. These diverse heroines united not by their creeds' specifics, but by the character strength to live and die by them.

Their fates contrast starkly. Joan faced trial and execution by the men she fought. Boudica's final battle ended in defeat and likely suicide to avoid capture. Nakano Takeko met her demise in a hail of bullets. Yet the Mino fared differently, their service ending when Dahomey modernized its military. Many lived to see old age.

These divergent fates remind us the warrior's path courts peril and often sacrifice. Yet their readiness to pay the ultimate price sets these women apart and cements their legend. By defying their eras' boundaries and daring to fight as bravely as any man, they expanded the realm of possibility and lit a way for generations.

In an age where equality remains a battle, their stories resound with relevance. They remind us of the extraordinary heights women can achieve when afforded opportunity. They challenge lingering gender role notions and limitations. Most of all, they stand as an eternal testament to unwavering conviction and indomitable human spirit.

The stories of Takeko, Boudica, Joan, and the Mino offer a stirring challenge. They call us to examine our own lives and consider - for what principles would we wage battle? Would we have the courage to defy expectations and fight for what we know is right?

By grappling with these questions, we honor their legacy. We recognize though from different worlds, they shared the warrior's spirit - martial excellence and steadfast conviction transcending era and culture, uniting bold pioneers across time.

As we navigate an uncertain world, we would do well to draw inspiration from these warrior women. They remind us greatness forges through struggle, that true strength lies in remaining true to oneself. They offer a model of courage facing overwhelming odds. Most of all, they remind us each of us has extraordinary potential within - we need only the boldness to seize it.

The Onna-Bugeisha Legacy

History celebrates tales of brave Samurai warriors and their courage in battle. However, equally formidable women warriors fought and died with valor matching their male counterparts. They were the Onna-bugeisha, the female warriors of feudal Japan. Among them, Nakano Takeko stands out with brilliance.

Takeko was born into the Samurai class during Japan's Edo period. Society confined women's roles to domestic duties under male authority. Yet, a few extraordinary women like Takeko dared to shatter the mold and chose the warrior's path. They dedicated themselves to martial arts and lived by the Bushido code.

From a young age, Takeko's father, a renowned Aizu Samurai, trained her in wielding the naginata with deadly skill. She became so proficient that she instructed other young women in the ways of war. However, her talents remained untested in battle during peacetime.

The Boshin War in 1868 changed that. When the war reached Aizu, Takeko knew her moment had arrived. She gathered female fighters and formed the Jōshitai, a women's combat unit. They rode out to engage the enemy.

On the battlefield, Takeko and her warriors stunned opponents with their ferocity. They launched surprise attacks and harried enemy flanks. Legendarily, Takeko led a charge into the imperial army's lines, cutting down foes with her naginata.

Despite bravery and skill, the Aizu forces faced a modern, Western-armed enemy. When defeat loomed, Takeko and her warriors chose to fight to the last breath, dying honorably as true Samurai.

Chapter 2: Chronicles of Courage

Takeko's Timeline

The journey of Nakano Takeko, from a promising young martial artist to a legendary female samurai, is a testament to unwavering dedication and an indomitable spirit. This timeline illuminates the pivotal moments that shaped her path, offering a glimpse into the extraordinary life of a woman who left an indelible mark on history.

Takeko was born in 1847 in Edo (present-day Tokyo) to a respected samurai family of the Aizu domain. From a young age, she began training in martial arts like kenjutsu (sword fighting) and naginatajutsu (naginata wielding) under her father and skilled instructors.

In 1853-1854, Commodore Matthew Perry of the U.S. Navy arrived in Japan, pressuring the country to open its ports to foreign trade. This event marked the beginning of the end of Japan's isolationist policy and set the stage for upheaval. The six-year-old Takeko witnessed growing tensions and political debates within the samurai class over how to respond.

From 1860-1863, Takeko continued her rigorous martial arts training, demonstrating exceptional skill and determination. She studied under the renowned swordsman Akaoka Daisuke, refining her techniques and deepening her understanding of the samurai code. Takeko also learned calligraphy and poetry, embracing cultural pursuits expected of a well-rounded samurai.

Between 1864-1867, political tensions rose as the Tokugawa shogunate's power waned and calls for imperial restoration grew louder. The Aizu domain, known for its martial tradition and loyalty to the shogunate, found itself at the center of the brewing conflict. Now in her late teens, Takeko took on a more active role, participating in discussions and preparing for possible war.

In 1868, the Boshin War, a civil war between the shogunate and imperial forces, erupted. Takeko's father, Nakano Heinai, led the Aizu forces in defense of their domain. Takeko and her sister Yūko formed a unit of female combatants known as the "Women's Army" (Jōshitai) to defend their homeland.

In September 1868, imperial forces laid siege to Aizuwakamatsu Castle, the stronghold of the Aizu domain. Takeko and the Women's Army took up frontline positions, engaging in fierce combat. Despite their valiant efforts, the Aizu forces were overwhelmed, and the castle fell after a month-long siege.

In October 1868, at the Battle of Aizu, Takeko led a final cavalry charge against the Imperial forces at Yanagi Bridge. Armed with a naginata, she fought fearlessly, cutting down several enemies before being fatally wounded by a gunshot. Rather than face capture, Takeko requested that her sister, Yūko, behead her to preserve her honor as a samurai.

Nakano Takeko's unwavering bravery and sacrifice in the face of overwhelming odds cemented her status as a legendary figure in Japanese history. Her story became an inspiration to generations of Japanese women, symbolizing the strength and resilience of the female spirit. Takeko's life and death embodied the core values of the samurai code

– loyalty, honor, and self-sacrifice – and served as a timeless reminder of the power of unwavering dedication to one's principles.

The Last Stand Analyzed

Legendary warriors often provide guiding lights, offering invaluable lessons on courage, strategy, and resilience. Nakano Takeko was one such luminary. By exploring her last battle, we uncover insights still relevant today.

We aim to analyze how Takeko's tactics and bravery during her final stand offer powerful lessons on resilience and leadership for modern warriors. To support this, we look to historical records of the Battle of Aizu, where Takeko and her female combatants, the Jōshitai, made their valiant last stand.

According to sources, Takeko led a cavalry charge against Imperial forces at Yanagi Bridge, wielding a naginata polearm. Despite overwhelming odds, Takeko and her warriors fought fearlessly until a gunshot felled her. Eyewitnesses describe Takeko cutting down several opponents like a whirlwind before falling.

Takeko's significance lies not just in individual bravery, but her strategic cavalry charge decision despite her forces' dire situation. This bold move impacted enemy psychology and inspired her troops. By leading from the front in direct combat, Takeko embodied samurai courage and self-sacrifice ideals, inspiring renewed vigor in her warriors.

Moreover, her willingness to charge despite near-certain defeat exemplifies resilience in adversity. While modern warriors may face different challenges, maintaining focus and determination remains crucial for leaders facing overwhelming odds.

Some scholars suggest Takeko's charge strategically bought time to regroup or negotiate surrender terms, adding complexity. This could demonstrate strategic thinking and adaptability amidst battle - vital skills for leaders.

Regardless of motivations, Takeko's example powerfully impacted morale. Facing defeat and losing their leader, the Jōshitai continued fighting bravely, with many taking their own lives rather than surrendering. This devotion testifies to Takeko's deep connection with her followers and how strong leadership rooted in courage can inspire extraordinary resilience.

Beyond the battlefield, Takeko challenged gender norms as a powerful female warrior symbol, inspiring generations of Japanese women. Her achievements highlighted women's strength and resilience, carrying relevance in modern gender equality discussions.

Studying Nakano Takeko provides valuable insights on resilience, adaptability, and leading by example - lessons highly relevant for modern warriors and leaders. Her pioneering role as a female warrior also reminds us of inclusion's importance for effective leadership.

Chapter 3: A Life of Duty and Honor

What Fuels a Warrior's Spirit?

What drives someone to embody the noble ideals of loyalty, duty, and honor? What fuels the warrior spirit? This profound question strikes at the heart of what it means to live with purpose and integrity. It invites us to explore the depths of human motivation and the wellspring from which true courage flows.

In today's world that often prioritizes self-interest and instant gratification, the concept of dedicating one's life to a higher code can seem old-fashioned or even naïve. Many might question why someone would choose a path of discipline, sacrifice, and potential danger when easier, more comfortable options exist. They may view the warrior's way as an outdated relic, out of touch with modern sensibilities.

But for individuals like Nakano Takeko, the young woman from a samurai family who became a formidable warrior and leader, the call to embody these ideals was undeniable. It emanated from a deep place within her spirit

– a place of unwavering conviction and clarity of purpose. For Takeko and others like her throughout history, the warrior's path wasn't a choice but a necessity – a way of life that aligned with their core values and gave meaning to their existence.

So what lies at the root of this drive? What fuels the fire that propels people to reach for something greater than themselves, to strive for excellence in service of a noble cause? I believe the answer is a combination of factors that shape the warrior spirit.

First, there is a profound sense of duty and responsibility. For samurai like Takeko, this duty was to their lord, clan, and the code of bushido that guided their actions. They understood they were part of something larger than themselves – a web of honor and obligation that demanded their utmost dedication. Today, this sense of duty might manifest as commitment to one's country, community, or personal principles. It's the understanding that we play a role and bear responsibility, even when it's difficult or dangerous.

Closely tied to this duty is fierce loyalty – to one's comrades, cause, and personal integrity. The warrior understands their strength comes not just from individual skills but from the bonds of trust and mutual support forged with others. They know they must be able to rely on fellow warriors just as others must be able to rely on them. This loyalty is a conscious choice to stand firm in the face of adversity, to have each other's backs no matter the cost.

Another key component is the drive for excellence and mastery. The true warrior is never satisfied with mediocrity but constantly pushes to be better, stronger, and more skilled. They understand that abilities may someday mean the difference between life and death, victory and defeat. So they train relentlessly, honing their minds and bodies into instruments of focused power. They strive not just for competence but excellence, knowing anything less betrays their duty and potential.

But perhaps most essential is a deep sense of honor and integrity that runs deeper than any external code or expectation. It's a fundamental commitment to doing what is right, even when it's hard, even when no one is watching. The warrior's true worth lies not in victories or reputation but in the quality of character. They strive to be honest, courageous, compassionate, and true to their word – because it's who they are at the core.

These values – duty, loyalty, excellence, integrity – form the bedrock of the warrior spirit. They provide the strength and resilience to face challenges that would break those of lesser resolve. And they imbue the warrior's actions with purpose and meaning transcending individual gain or glory.

Yet the path of the warrior is not an easy one. It demands sacrifice, discipline, and willingness to face deepest fears. It requires courage to stand up for what is right, even when consequences may be dire. And it calls for mental and physical toughness that can only be forged through relentless training and unyielding dedication.

For Nakano Takeko and other warrior women throughout history, there were additional barriers. They faced not only the warrior lifestyle's inherent challenges but also prejudices and limitations from a society viewing women as inferior or incapable. Their very presence on the battlefield or in the dojo defied the roles and restrictions imposed on them.

In rising to meet these challenges and proving their mettle, these women warriors embodied the highest samurai ideals while expanding possibilities for what women could achieve. They shattered stereotypes and paved the way for future generations, demonstrating that courage, skill, and indomitable spirit know no gender.

While most of us will never charge into battle, we all face challenges and obstacles demanding our best. We all have duties and responsibilities calling us to rise above self-interest and serve a greater good. By cultivating the warrior spirit's values – duty, loyalty, the drive for excellence, and unwavering commitment to integrity – we tap into a source of strength and resilience serving us well in any endeavor.

Embodying these ideals is a lifelong practice requiring ongoing reflection, discipline, and willingness to learn and grow. It means being honest about strengths and weaknesses while constantly striving for improvement. It means surrounding ourselves with others who share our values and support us as we support them.

Ultimately, the warrior spirit transcends individual achievement or glory. It's about dedicating ourselves to something larger and striving to make a positive difference. It's having courage to stand up for our beliefs, even when difficult, and inspiring others through our example.

In an often chaotic world, the warrior's steadfast commitment and spirit can serve as a beacon of hope – a call to action. By embodying these timeless values, we tap into the strength and purpose sustaining humanity's greatest heroes. And in doing so, we face our challenges with courage and grace while contributing to a better, more just world for all.

Takeko's Training: The Making of a Samurai

In the heart of 19th-century Japan, as a young girl, Nakano Takeko embarked on an extraordinary journey. Born into the proud samurai heritage of the Aizu clan, she was no ordinary child. From an early age, Takeko displayed fierce determination and an innate talent for the martial arts. This is the story of her rigorous training that forged her into one of history's most legendary female samurai.

To understand the significance of Takeko's training, we must consider the context of her time. In the mid-1800s, Japan underwent tremendous upheaval as the feudal system crumbled. The traditional role of the samurai eroded, and society expected women to conform to strict norms as dutiful wives and mothers - not warriors. But Takeko's family, the Nakanos, recognized her potential and encouraged her warrior path, defying societal pressures.

Takeko's training commenced at age six under her father Nakano Heinai, a skilled samurai himself. Heinai recognized the warrior spirit within his daughter and fanned that flame. He instilled the basics of martial arts: stances, strikes, and the discipline to master body and mind. Takeko embraced her training with a passion that surprised even her father, practicing tirelessly to hone her techniques.

As Takeko grew older, her training intensified. She mastered the sword, bow, spear - the three primary samurai weapons. She studied strategy, tactics, and the philosophy of bushido, the warrior's code that guided loyalty, honor, and self-sacrifice. One of her most significant skills became naginatajutsu, the art of wielding the naginata, a long pole with a curved blade. Traditionally a woman's weapon for home defense, the naginata became Takeko's symbol of defiance against gender limitations. She mastered it with unrivaled skill.

But Takeko's training transcended the physical realm. She delved into the spiritual and mental aspects through Zen Buddhism, meditation, calligraphy, and poetry. She cultivated her intellect and creativity, embodying the ideal of the well-rounded samurai.

As adulthood neared, Takeko's skills faced the ultimate test: mock battles and tournaments where she proved her mettle. Her reputation as a formidable warrior grew. But her greatest challenge loomed in 1868 when civil war erupted. The Aizu clan, loyal to the shogun, found itself outmatched. Takeko, now a fully-fledged samurai, knew her duty. She gathered female warriors trained in the naginata and led them into battle, fighting bravely until outnumbered and outgunned. Takeko fell, her naginata broken, her body riddled with bullets – but her unbroken spirit endured.

Takeko's story testifies to the power of dedication, discipline, and the pursuit of excellence. Through her training, she transformed from a young girl into a legend inspiring generations. She shattered gender barriers, proving a warrior's spirit knows no bounds.

But Takeko's legacy transcends martial prowess. It embodies the values she lived: loyalty, honor, and self-sacrifice. In a world celebrating selfishness, she reminds us to live for something greater than ourselves. She challenges us to find our path and pursue our passions with the same fiery dedication she brought to her training.

Of course, we must recognize the historical context and flaws of the samurai way, with its rigid hierarchies and emphasis on blind loyalty. And the glorification of martial prowess can prove problematic today. But these limitations do not diminish the core lessons from Takeko's journey.

Ultimately, Takeko's training forged an unbreakable spirit that could withstand any adversity while staying true to her values. It was about becoming the best version of herself in body, mind, and heart. This essence of the samurai way resonates powerfully across time. As we embrace perseverance, integrity, and the courage to stand for our beliefs, we keep Takeko's legacy alive, joining a lineage of warriors stretching through the ages to inspire generations to come.

Shattering Stereotypes: Takeko Vs. Gender Norms

In 19th-century Japan, society rigidly defined men's and women's roles. Men, especially samurai, embodied courage, strength, and martial prowess. Women were confined to the domestic sphere, valued for managing households and raising children. Against this backdrop, Nakano Takeko emerged as a remarkable anomaly - a woman who defied every societal norm to become one of history's most legendary female samurai.

To understand the magnitude of Takeko's defiance, we must examine the gender roles of her time. Samurai families expected women to uphold the "good wife, wise mother" (ryōsai kenbo) ideal. They were to be demure, obedient, and focused on domestic duties. Martial arts, politics, and warfare remained strictly male domains. Women might learn basic naginata self-defense to protect the home when husbands were away.

Takeko shattered these norms from childhood. Instead of needlework and tea ceremonies, she devoted herself to martial arts. Her father, recognizing her potential, trained her alongside male samurai. Takeko mastered the sword, spear, bow, and naginata with unrivaled skill. She delved into military strategy and philosophy. In a society prizing conformity, Takeko unapologetically stood out.

Numerous aspects of Takeko's life defied gender norms. First, her pursuit of martial arts was radical. Women were not supposed to be warriors or find fulfillment outside the home. By dedicating herself to the way of the samurai, Takeko challenged fundamental assumptions about a woman's place.

Moreover, Takeko's mastery of the naginata was subversive. Traditionally a woman's weapon for home defense, Takeko transformed the naginata into a symbol of female martial prowess. She wielded it with such skill that she matched male samurai, reclaiming the naginata as a tool of women's empowerment.

The implications of Takeko's defiance are profound. On a personal level, she achieved rare self-actualization by living authentically, not society's prescribed life for her. She found fulfillment in the martial arts, the way of the samurai, and defending her clan and beliefs. In a world demanding conformity, Takeko was unapologetically herself.

A Legacy of Honor: Preserving Samurai Values

Takeko's life stood as a powerful testament to staying true to one's convictions despite overwhelming societal pressure. She defied gender norms by embodying the samurai values of courage, discipline, and skill as fully as any man. In doing so, Takeko challenged the foundations of Japan's patriarchal society.

However, her defiance extended beyond just gender roles. Takeko aimed to preserve the essence of the samurai spirit during Japan's rapid modernization and Westernization in the late 19th century Meiji Restoration period. As the country embraced new technologies, political systems, and cultural influences, many feared losing the traditional samurai values.

Takeko recognized this threat and made it her mission to ensure the core samurai way - loyalty, honor, discipline, and self-sacrifice -

endured. She understood these values were universal principles that could guide any individual, regardless of gender.

To preserve these values, she took innovative leadership and martial arts instruction approaches. Takeko knew passing on techniques alone wasn't enough - she needed to instill the samurai spirit in her students. In training, she emphasized the mental and spiritual dimensions as much as the physical. Takeko taught her students to cultivate inner strength, face fear with courage, and maintain composure under pressure. She instilled in them fierce loyalty to their clan and readiness to sacrifice their lives for a greater cause.

Takeko's teachings resonated deeply with students of both genders. They saw her as a living embodiment of the samurai ideal, a beacon of honor in changing times. Her female students found empowerment in her example, realizing gender posed no barrier to embodying samurai values.

Takeko's influence extended far beyond her immediate students. As her reputation grew, other instructors adopted her effective training methods for forging not just skilled fighters, but principled individuals. Even after her death in battle, her legendary tale of courage and sacrifice inspired generations as a reminder of honorable living and dying.

In preserving the samurai way, Takeko demonstrated its timeless relevance and ability to guide individuals through any era's challenges. She showed the samurai path wasn't about rigid external codes, but cultivating inner strength, integrity, and unwavering commitment to principles.

Today, in a Japan unrecognizable to Takeko, her legacy endures. In dojos, boardrooms, schools, and homes, the values she embodied - courage, discipline, loyalty, self-sacrifice - continue guiding and inspiring. They remind us that living with honor is possible in any circumstance.

Takeko's life testifies to the power of individual spirit. Through conviction and integrity, one person can leave an indelible historical mark. She challenged limits imposed by society, expanding the realm of possibility for all who followed.

Ultimately, Takeko's greatest legacy may not be martial prowess or her Boshin War role, but how she lived - with unflinching commitment to values, a warrior's compassionate and wise spirit. In upheaval, she was constant, reminding us what it means to live with honor.

As Japan navigates modern challenges, Takeko's example remains relevant. Her life calls us to find our path, stay true to convictions, and strive to live with integrity. It reminds us the samurai way isn't past relic, but living path open to all courageous enough to walk it.

Honoring Takeko's legacy honors the best in ourselves - the part aspiring to live with courage, serve with loyalty, and face challenges with a warrior's unwavering spirit. Takeko Nakano was more than historical figure - she was and remains an inspiration, a guide star for all seeking a life of purpose and honor.

Chapter 4: Takeko's Era

Understanding the forces that shaped Nakano Takeko's life and the samurai values she embodied requires exploring the historical landscape of her era. This timeline illuminates significant events and cultural shifts that influenced not only Takeko's path but Japan's trajectory as well. By tracing this rich tapestry, we gain a deeper appreciation for the context that cultivated Takeko's unwavering sense of duty and courage.

Our journey begins in the early 19th century during a relatively peaceful and stable period under the Tokugawa shogunate. Born in 1847 to a samurai family in the Aizu domain, Takeko spent her formative years immersed in warrior traditions passed down for generations. From a young age, she would have learned the core tenets of bushido, the way of the warrior, emphasizing loyalty, honor, and selfless service.

While Takeko trained in martial arts and absorbed the samurai ethos, winds of change stirred across Japan. In 1853, the arrival of Commodore Matthew Perry's Black Ships marked a pivotal moment when the United States pressured Japan to open its ports to foreign trade. This intrusion by Western powers shook Japanese society, challenging the isolationist policies that had prevailed for over two centuries.

As Japan grappled with ending its seclusion, significant events unfolded:

- 1854: The Convention of Kanagawa established diplomatic relations between Japan and the United States.

- 1858: The Treaty of Amity and Commerce opened additional Japanese ports to American trade and granted extraterritoriality to foreign residents.

- 1860s: The sonnō jōi ("revere the emperor, expel the barbarians") movement gained momentum, advocating for restoring imperial rule and expelling foreigners.

Against this backdrop of political upheaval and social unrest, Takeko witnessed the increasing tensions between those preserving traditional values and those embracing Western influences. The Aizu clan, known for its loyalty to the Tokugawa shogunate, found itself at the center of this maelstrom.

As the call for imperial restoration grew louder in the 1860s, it culminated in the pivotal Boshin War of 1868-1869. This civil war pitted the Tokugawa shogunate and its allies, including the Aizu clan, against imperial forces seeking to overthrow the feudal system. In this crucible of conflict, Takeko's unwavering duty and martial prowess were forged and tested.

Drawing upon her samurai training and driven by fierce loyalty to her clan and its cause, Takeko took up arms to defend Aizu against the imperial army. Despite overwhelming odds, she fought with skill and courage, earning respect from comrades and enemies alike. Her leadership and bravery in battle testified to the enduring samurai spirit, even as the world around her changed irrevocably.

Tragically, Takeko would not live to see the war's outcome or the profound transformations that followed. Her death became a symbol of the samurai's commitment to duty and honor, even in the face of certain defeat.

After the Boshin War, the Tokugawa shogunate was abolished, and the Meiji Restoration ushered in rapid modernization and Westernization. The samurai class was officially dissolved, and many traditional privileges and customs associated with this warrior elite were swept away. But as Japan embraced a new identity and charted a course toward becoming a modern nation-state, the samurai legacy endured. The values of loyalty, self-discipline, and selfless service found new expressions in the emerging social and political order. The spirit of bushido continued to shape Japanese culture and consciousness as the country navigated the 20th century's challenges.

For Takeko Nakano, whose life tragically ended too soon, this historical tapestry provides rich context for understanding her choices and actions. Born into upheaval and a samurai family steeped in warrior traditions, Takeko embodied the highest ideals of duty and courage in the face of overwhelming adversity. Her brief story stands as a powerful testament to the enduring human spirit and timeless values that guide us through even the darkest times.

Reflecting on Takeko's era and the historical forces that shaped her world reminds us of our profound interconnectedness with history's larger currents. We see how individuals' choices and actions like Takeko's can reverberate through time, leaving an indelible mark on a nation's collective memory and identity.

More than a century and a half after her death, Takeko Nakano's legacy continues to inspire and resonate worldwide. Her unwavering commitment to duty, her fierce loyalty to clan and cause, and her ultimate sacrifice in battle have become enduring symbols of the samurai spirit and timeless values transcending culture and era.

In our rapidly changing world, where old certainties are constantly challenged and redefined, Takeko's story serves as a reminder of staying true to core values and principles. It encourages us to cultivate the same sense of duty, courage, and selflessness that guided her life and face our own challenges with unwavering spirit and determination.

As we navigate the complexities of the present and uncertainties of the future, let us draw strength and inspiration from the historical tapestry that shaped Takeko's era. Let us embrace the timeless wisdom of the samurai, not as a relic of the past, but as a living guide for forging purposeful, meaningful lives of unbreakable spirit. In doing so, we honor Nakano Takeko's memory and all who came before us, weaving our unique threads into humanity's ever-unfolding tapestry.

The Power of Example: Takeko's Influence Verified

Nakano Takeko's life and actions have profoundly impacted history. Her honor, courage, and sacrifice still resonate as a powerful symbol across generations. To truly understand her example's profound impact, we must examine tangible evidence of how she shaped individuals, society, and culture long after her tragic battlefield death.

The central idea is clear: Takeko's unwavering commitment to samurai values, her fearless leadership against overwhelming odds, and her ultimate sacrifice inspired countless others to live with integrity, bravery, and purpose. However, we must look at concrete proof that verifies her lasting influence.

One compelling testament to Takeko's impact is the reverence she commands in her homeland of Aizu. In Aizuwakamatsu, a monument honors her at the site of her final battle, serving as a tangible reminder of her courage and the Aizu clan's sacrifices. This memorial's endurance for over a century, drawing admirers from across Japan, speaks volumes about the enduring power of her example.

Moreover, the Aizu Clan School, where Takeko honed her martial skills and absorbed the samurai ethos, still operates as a living embodiment of the values she upheld. Students continue learning the naginata she wielded with deadly precision and studying the bushido principles that guided her life. The school's commitment to preserving these practices testifies to her legacy's enduring relevance.

Beyond local tributes, countless literary works, films, and artistic depictions celebrate Takeko's life and deeds. From the earliest accounts of her bravery in the Aizu Boshin Senshi to recent portrayals in popular media, her story has captured imaginations and inspired generations.

For instance, Yamamoto Shugoro's novel "Yae no Sakura" featured a fictionalized Takeko and fellow warrior Yamamoto Yaeko. This bestseller, later adapted into a TV series, brought Takeko's tale to wide audiences, sparking renewed interest in her life and the samurai values she embodied. That her story still resonates with modern readers and viewers powerfully indicates its enduring appeal and relevance.

But Takeko's influence extends beyond popular culture. Her example inspired and empowered women in Japan and beyond. In a male-dominated society, her story reminds us of the strength, courage, and leadership women can demonstrate, even facing incredible adversity.

Scholars and activists increasingly recognize female warriors and leaders like Takeko throughout Japanese history. As they uncover these overlooked contributions, Takeko's story challenges traditional gender roles and expectations, proving her example's enduring power.

Most importantly, countless individuals draw strength and inspiration from Takeko's story as they face challenges. From World War II soldiers to today's activists and leaders, her unwavering values and willingness to sacrifice guided them through adversity, reminding them of courage, integrity, and selflessness' power.

One example is Hiroo Onoda, a Japanese soldier who fought for decades after WWII ended. When asked about his incredible devotion, Onoda cited samurai warriors like Takeko, whose unwavering loyalty inspired his perseverance long after others surrendered.

Onoda's story exemplifies how Takeko's legacy touched and transformed lives. From the young woman finding courage against injustice, to the soldier drawing battlefield strength from her example, to the many living with greater purpose after being inspired by her story, Takeko's influence shapes our world.

The evidence of Nakano Takeko's enduring impact is compelling. Through monuments, institutions, literature, art, and transformed lives, her legacy continues inspiring new generations to live with courage, honor, and purpose.

By examining this evidence, we move beyond legend and gain a deeper appreciation for the tangible ways Takeko's life shaped the world. We can draw the same strength and inspiration countless others have from her shining example of living a principled life with purpose and resolve, even against overwhelming odds.

This is Nakano Takeko's true legacy - a living, breathing example of honor, sacrifice, and the unbreakable human spirit that will continue inspiring us as long as we believe in courage, integrity, and purpose's enduring power.

Chapter 5: Recorded Jōshitai

The historical records about the Jōshitai (Women's Army) primarily focus on Nakano Takeko and a few other notable members. However, comprehensive lists of all members are sparse, and detailed biographies of each member are not extensively documented. Here are the other members known through historical records:

1. Yamamoto Yae (Yamamoto Yaeko)
2. Nakano Yuko
3. Niijima Yae

Yamamoto Yae: A Trailblazer in Wartime Valor and Postwar Reconstruction

Yamamoto Yae, also known later as Niijima Yae, stands as a remarkable figure in Japanese history. Born in 1845 in Aizu, she was the daughter of Yamamoto Gonpachi, a gunnery instructor for the Aizu domain. Her upbringing in a samurai family, coupled with the progressive educational opportunities her father provided, laid the foundation for her extraordinary life, marked by wartime bravery and significant contributions to education and healthcare in Japan's Meiji era.

From an early age, Yae exhibited a strong interest in military skills, particularly in the use of firearms, which was uncommon for women in her time. Under her father's guidance, she trained rigorously in marksmanship and gunnery. This training was not merely a hobby but a profound preparation for the tumultuous events that would shape her destiny.

The Boshin War brought Yae's martial skills to the forefront. Yae, determined to protect her home and family, took an active role in the defense of Aizu.

Yae's expertise in firearms made her a valuable asset. She operated cannons and rifles with remarkable precision, earning a reputation as a sharpshooter. Her presence on the battlefield was not merely symbolic; she was deeply involved in the strategic defense efforts, standing shoulder to shoulder with male samurai. Her courage and resilience during the siege became legendary, embodying the samurai spirit of unwavering dedication and honor.

Following the fall of Aizu, Yae's life took a transformative turn. She moved to Kyoto, where she encountered Joseph Hardy Neesima, an influential Christian missionary and educator. Their meeting marked the beginning of a significant partnership, both personally and professionally. They married in 1876, and Yae adopted the name Niijima Yae.

Embracing Christianity, Yae became deeply involved in the educational and social reform movements that were reshaping Japan during the Meiji era. Together with her husband, she co-founded Doshisha University in Kyoto. The institution aimed to provide a modern, Western-style education, emphasizing ethical and moral development. Yae's role in the establishment and growth of Doshisha University was crucial, as she championed the integration of Western educational principles with traditional Japanese values.

Yae's dedication to public service extended beyond education. During the Satsuma Rebellion in 1877, she volunteered as a nurse, applying her knowledge and skills to care for the wounded. Her efforts during this conflict highlighted the critical role of women in healthcare, setting a precedent for future generations of female nurses in Japan.

Yae's involvement in nursing was not limited to wartime. She continued to advocate for the improvement of healthcare services and the professionalization of nursing, contributing to the broader social reforms of the Meiji era.

Yamamoto Yae's legacy is multifaceted. She is remembered as a fierce warrior who defied traditional gender roles, a dedicated educator who helped lay the foundations for modern education in Japan, and a compassionate nurse who served her country in times of need. Her life story is a testament to resilience, adaptability, and the profound impact one individual can have on society.

Yae's contributions to Japan's cultural and educational reforms during the Meiji Restoration era continue to inspire. Her blend of martial prowess and compassionate service underscores the enduring importance of courage, education, and social responsibility. As a pioneer in multiple fields, Yamamoto Yae's life serves as a powerful reminder of the potential for individuals to drive significant change, regardless of the challenges they face.

Nakano Yuko: The Unsung Heroine of the Jōshitai

Nakano Yuko is a less-documented yet significant figure in Japanese history, best known for her involvement in the Boshin War and her role in the Jōshitai (Women's Army). As the younger sister of the celebrated Nakano Takeko, Yuko's story is intertwined with themes of loyalty, bravery, and the struggle for survival in a time of profound political upheaval.

Born into a samurai family in the mid-19th century, Nakano Yuko was raised in the Aizu Domain, a region known for its strong martial traditions. The Nakano family ensured that Yuko, like her sister Takeko, received rigorous training in the martial arts, including the use of the naginata, a traditional Japanese pole weapon. This training was crucial in preparing her for the challenges she would face during the Boshin War.

During the Battle of Aizu, Yuko fought alongside her sister and the other members of the Jōshitai. The battle was fierce, and the Jōshitai's involvement provided a significant morale boost to the Aizu defenders.

One of the most poignant moments in Yuko's life came when her sister, Nakano Takeko, was fatally wounded in combat. In an act of profound loyalty and courage, Yuko complied with her sister's request. She then buried Takeko's head under a pine tree at the Hokai-ji Temple to honor her sister's final wishes and protect her dignity.

Following the fall of Aizu, Yuko's life entered a quieter phase. The details of her later years are less documented, but it is known that she survived the conflict and lived on to preserve the memory of her sister and the Jōshitai. Yuko's actions during the battle, particularly her fulfillment of Takeko's final request, highlight her deep sense of duty and familial loyalty.

While Nakano Yuko did not achieve the same level of fame as her sister, her contributions to the defense of Aizu and her role in the Jōshitai are integral to the narrative of female valor during the Boshin War. Her story, though less celebrated, is a testament to the bravery and resilience of the women who fought alongside their male counterparts in a time of great crisis.

Nakano Yuko's life and actions during the Boshin War exemplify the often-overlooked heroism of women in Japanese history. Her courage in the face of overwhelming odds, her loyalty to her sister, and her participation in the Jōshitai's defense of Aizu serve as powerful reminders of the important roles women played in shaping Japan's past. Yuko's legacy, while quieter than that of her sister, remains an essential part of the rich tapestry of the samurai tradition and the history of the Meiji Restoration.

Niijima Yae (Yamamoto Yaeko): A Pioneer in Female Bravery and Education

Niijima Yae, also known as Yamamoto Yaeko, was a remarkable figure in Japanese history, renowned for her exceptional courage during the Boshin War and her significant contributions to education and nursing in the Meiji era. Born in 1845 in Aizu, Yae was the daughter of Yamamoto Gonpachi, a gunnery instructor for the Aizu domain. This early exposure to military training and firearms set the stage for her later achievements.

From a young age, Yae was determined to break through the societal constraints placed on women in feudal Japan. She learned how to handle firearms and developed a deep interest in Western-style gunnery, which was a rarity for women of her time. Her father's position allowed her access to education and training that was typically reserved for men, nurturing her skills and preparing her for the challenges ahead.

During the Boshin War (1868-1869), Yae's martial prowess came to the forefront. Yae took an active role in the defense of Aizu, demonstrating her expertise in gunnery and her indomitable spirit. She is famously known for her sharpshooting skills and her determination to fight alongside the male samurai.

Yae's involvement in the battle was not merely symbolic; she played a critical role in manning the cannons and rifles, standing her ground even as the situation grew dire. Her courage and resilience made her a legendary figure in Aizu, earning her a place among the ranks of samurai women who defied traditional gender roles. Despite the eventual fall of Aizu, Yae survived the conflict and her legacy as a warrior was firmly established.

Following the Boshin War, Yae's life took a transformative turn. She moved to Kyoto, where she encountered Joseph Hardy Neesima, an American-educated Japanese Christian missionary. Yae and Neesima married in 1876, and she adopted the name Niijima Yae. Her marriage to Neesima marked the beginning of a new chapter in her life, one focused on education and social reform.

Yae and Neesima co-founded Doshisha University in Kyoto, a significant milestone in Japan's educational landscape. Doshisha University aimed to provide a modern, Western-style education, and Yae played an essential role in its establishment and development. She embraced Christianity, which influenced her approach to education and social work, emphasizing compassion, moral integrity, and the importance of serving others.

In addition to her contributions to education, Yae became a pioneering figure in nursing.

During the Satsuma Rebellion (1877), she volunteered as a nurse, applying her knowledge and skills to care for the wounded. Her efforts in nursing highlighted the critical role of women in healthcare and set a precedent for future generations.

Niijima Yae's life is a testament to her resilience, adaptability, and commitment to progress. From her early days as a warrior defending Aizu to her later years as an educator and nurse, Yae continually broke barriers and challenged societal norms. Her legacy is multifaceted; she is remembered not only as a symbol of female bravery but also as a pioneer in education and healthcare during a transformative period in Japanese history.

Yae's story continues to inspire, embodying the spirit of perseverance and the impact one individual can have on society. Her contributions to the Meiji Restoration's cultural and educational reforms are a reminder of the enduring importance of courage, education, and social responsibility.

The Jōshitai's members, led by figures like Nakano Takeko and Yamamoto Yae, displayed extraordinary courage and determination during the Battle of Aizu. Their stories, though not all extensively recorded, contribute to the rich tapestry of Japan's history, showcasing the indomitable spirit of women warriors in a time of great upheaval and change. The legacy of these women continues to inspire and is commemorated through various historical and cultural narratives in Japan.

Conclusion

Nakano Takeko's life and legacy and that of the Jōshitai offer profound lessons that transcend time and culture. Her unwavering devotion to the samurai bushido code, fearless leadership amid adversity, and ultimate sacrifice continue to inspire and guide us today.

The key principles that defined Takeko's life include:

1. Unwavering loyalty and devotion: From a young age, Takeko dedicated herself fully to the Aizu clan and samurai values like honor, loyalty, and duty. This commitment to a higher cause gave her life purpose beyond individual desires. We too can cultivate devotion by identifying causes, values, or principles that truly matter. Having a higher purpose infuses life with meaning and strength to persevere through challenges.

2. Fearless leadership amid adversity: During the Battle of Aizu, Takeko led female warriors into a desperate charge against overwhelming odds. Instead of surrendering,

she rallied her comrades with unflinching courage. We will face obstacles that test our resolve. In those moments, we can draw from Takeko's example and lead with conviction, mobilizing others despite uncertain victory.

3. Upholding honor and integrity: For Takeko and samurai, honor and moral integrity were paramount - more important than personal gain or self-preservation. Today's world often values expediency over ethics. Takeko reminds us to live by higher standards: keep our word, stand up for our beliefs, and act with moral courage.

4. Disciplined pursuit of excellence: Takeko's warrior skills resulted from rigorous, disciplined training over years. Achieving excellence in any pursuit requires the same commitment: setting ambitious goals, steady effort, and sacrifice. With Takeko's dedication, we can develop mastery, unlock potential, and find greater fulfillment.

5. Selfless sacrifice: Ultimately, Takeko sacrificed her life to defend her clan's ideals. Her selflessness challenges us to think beyond self-interest and consider how to serve a

greater good through our actions - by volunteering, fighting injustice, or simply supporting loved ones.

Nakano Takeko embodied honor, courage and principled living against all odds. By embracing her core values, we too can lead lives of profound meaning and positive impact on the world around us.